JOHN ADAMS
OPERA CHORUSES

VOLUME 1

CHORUSES FROM
EL NIÑO
THE GOSPEL ACCORDING TO THE OTHER MARY

EDITED BY GRANT GERSHON

HENDON MUSIC

www.boosey.com

The first time I met John Adams I was playing piano rehearsals for *Nixon in China*. The year was 1990 and I remember vividly both the unbridled joy of discovering his work for the first time and the utter terror that my counting would go awry, and I'd fall into one of those infamous "John Adams holes" where one careens full-bore into a beat of (intended) silence. John was extraordinarily kind to me in those rehearsals and he clearly had a sense of how crazy it is to corral an entire orchestra's worth of activity into 10 fingers! That began a long and treasured friendship, and I have an enduring love, based on those early experiences, of hearing John's operas and oratorios played on the piano.

Over the past 30 years I've played, conducted, and in several cases, premiered John's works with continued joy and (maybe slightly) less terror. As a pianist and conductor with a deep love of choirs I've often wished that there was more music of John's available to choral ensembles. John seems to pour heart and soul into the choruses of his large-scale works and so it has been frustrating that only those choral ensembles lucky enough to be associated with a symphony orchestra or opera company have heretofore had access to this great repertoire. I'm therefore delighted that these newly transcribed versions of some of John's greatest choruses will open up his music to many more choral ensembles and pianists.

I'm hugely grateful to Zizi Mueller for envisioning and championing this undertaking, and to Maggie Heskin for shepherding it through to completion. We recently "test drove" several of these transcriptions in concert with the Los Angeles Master Chorale and I'm deeply indebted for both the brilliant playing and the honest feedback from our four rock star pianists—Gloria Cheng, Lisa Edwards, Bryan Pezzone and Vicki Ray. Most of all I am in awe of Chitose Okashiro for wrestling the unbridled inventiveness of John's orchestral writing into 88 keys, two hands and 10 digits! These transcriptions are imaginative, colorful, and of course fantastically virtuosic. I hope that through them and through this edition John Adams' great choral music will resonate with adventurous choral ensembles far and wide!

—Grant Gershon

CONTENTS

I Sing of a Maiden
from El Niño

Libretto based on original sources, arranged by
PETER SELLARS and **JOHN ADAMS**

Piano reduction by
CHITOSE OKASHIRO

Music by
JOHN ADAMS

979-0-051-48572-7

Printed 2020

* Countertenor 3 may sing also, deleting phrases that go out of range.

gradually take the pedal away

FOR WITH GOD NOTHING SHALL BE IMPOSSIBLE
from EL NIÑO

Libretto based on original sources, arranged by
PETER SELLARS and **JOHN ADAMS**

Piano reduction by
CHITOSE OKASHIRO

Music by
JOHN ADAMS

* Sing full rhythmic values of each note. Do not treat as staccato.

** Sing at written range.

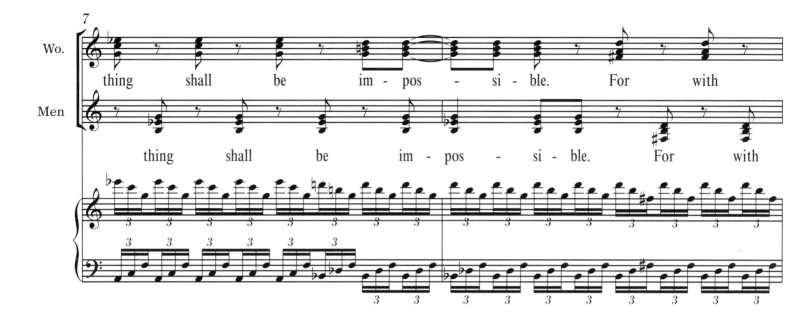

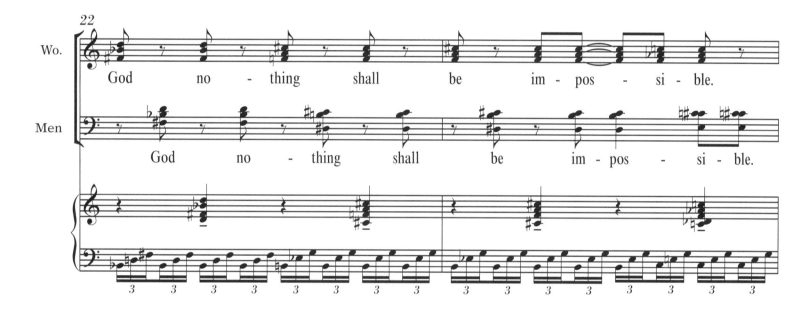

Woe Unto Them That Call Evil Good
from El Niño

Libretto based on original sources, arranged by
PETER SELLARS and **JOHN ADAMS**

Music by
JOHN ADAMS

Piano reduction by
CHITOSE OKASHIRO

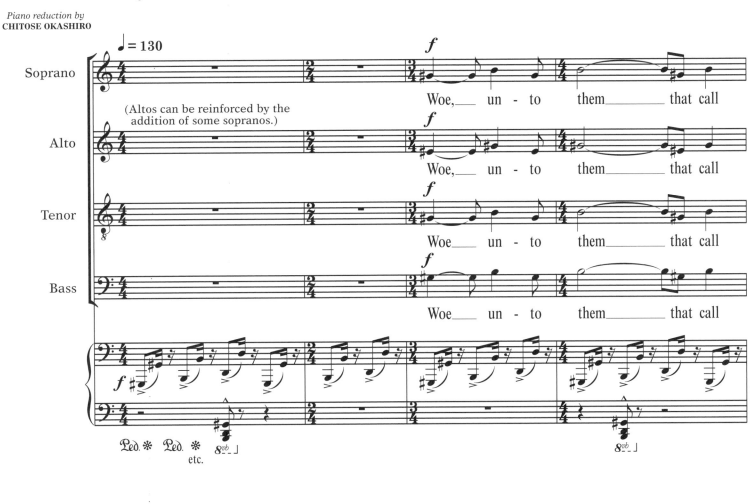

AND HE SLEW ALL THE CHILDREN
from EL NIÑO

Libretto based on original sources, arranged by
PETER SELLARS and **JOHN ADAMS**

Piano reduction by
CHITOSE OKASHIRO

Music by
JOHN ADAMS

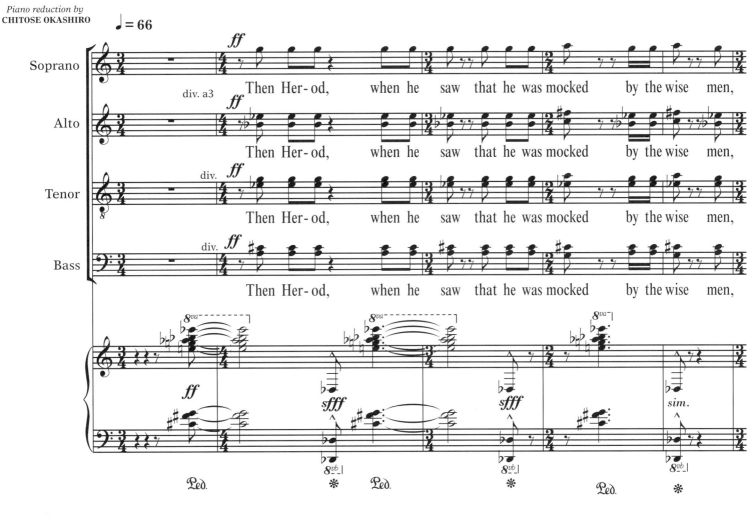

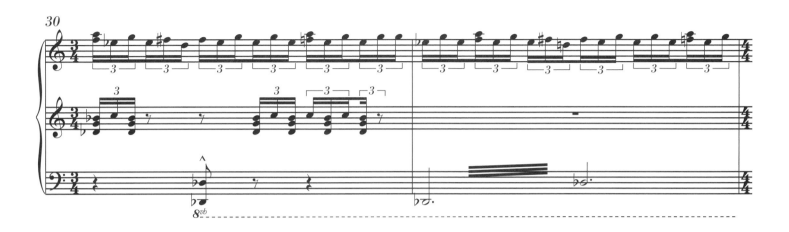

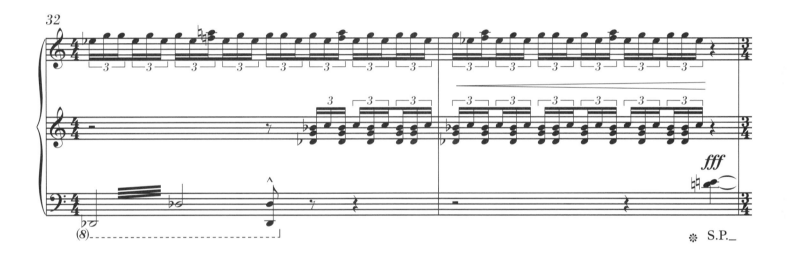

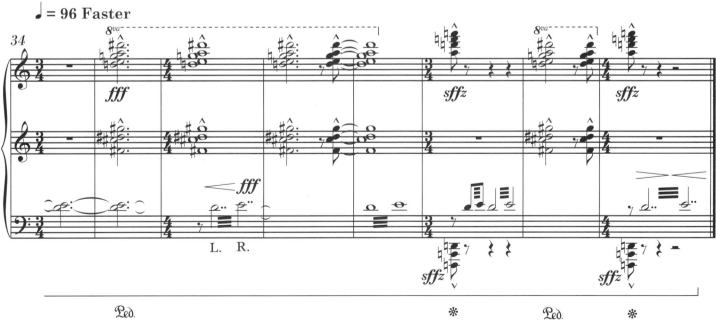

EN UN DÍA DE AMOR
from THE GOSPEL ACCORDING TO THE OTHER MARY

Libretto compiled by
PETER SELLARS

Piano reduction by
CHITOSE OKASHIRO

Music by
JOHN ADAMS

* The English translation is not to be sung
** Tenors sing only when range is comfortable

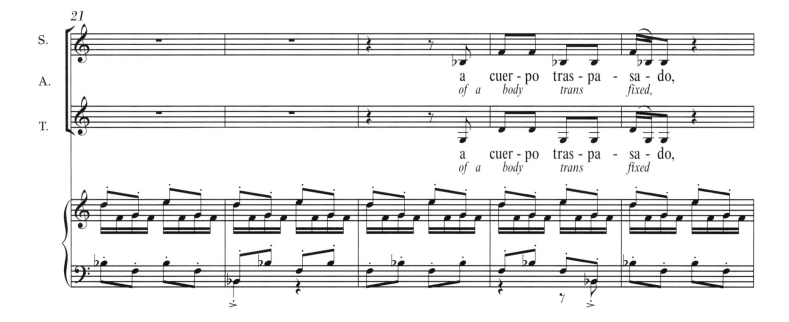

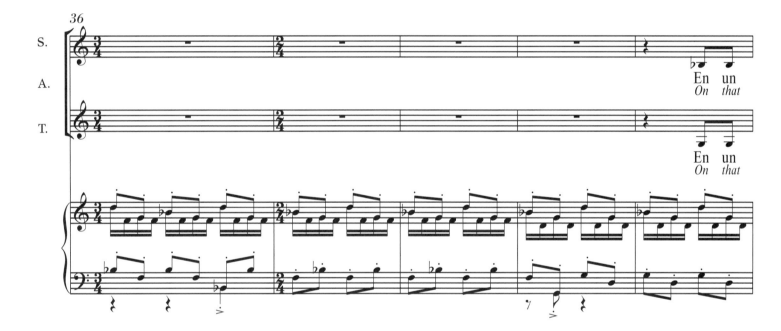

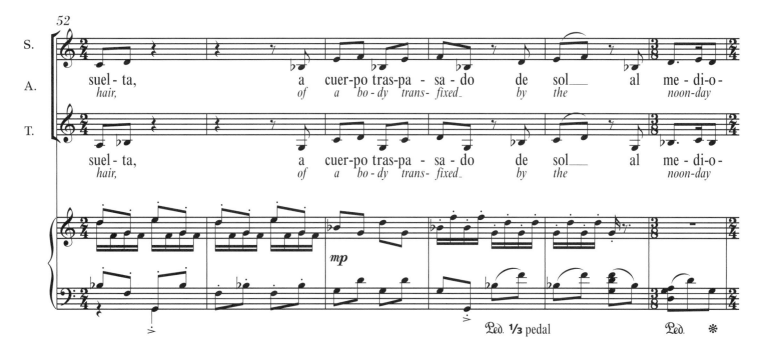

di-cha, y en-ce-rra-ba la di-cha, la di-cha
happiness, *and* *it* *en-circled* *hap-pi-ness* *hap-pi-ness*

di-cha, y en-ce-rra-ba la di-cha, la di-cha
happiness, *and* *it* *en-circled* *hap-pi-ness* *hap-pi-ness*

di-cha, y en-ce-rra-ba la di-cha, la di-cha
happiness, *and* *it* *en-circled* *hap-pi-ness* *hap-pi-ness*

co-mo los la-bios en-cie-rran un be- so.
as *lips* *en-cir-cle* *a* *kiss.*

co-mo los la-bios en-cie-rran un be- so.
as *lips* *en-cir-cle* *a* *kiss.*

co-mo los la-bios en-cie-rran un be- so.
as *lips* *en-cir-cle* *a* *kiss.*

✳ 🜊 full pedal

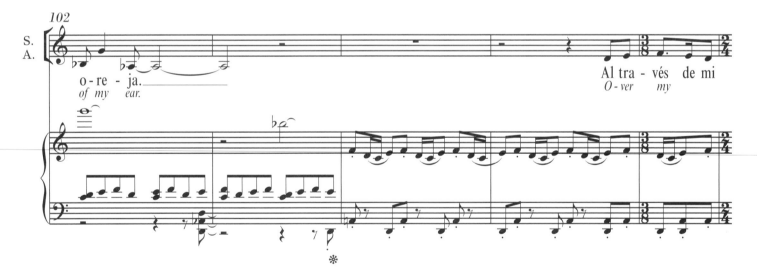

* Optional cut: skip m. 179 through m. 207

-DE

℘ed.

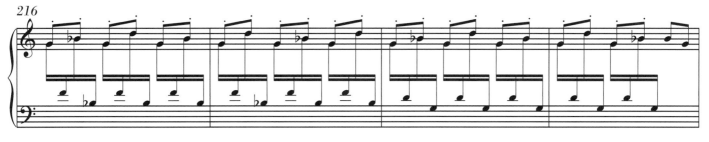

✳

Relax tempo very slightly

DROP DOWN, YE HEAVENS
from THE GOSPEL ACCORDING
TO THE OTHER MARY

Libretto compiled by
PETER SELLARS

Music by
JOHN ADAMS

Piano reduction by
CHITOSE OKASHIRO

* Strophe marks indicate normal stress. Do not accent heavily.

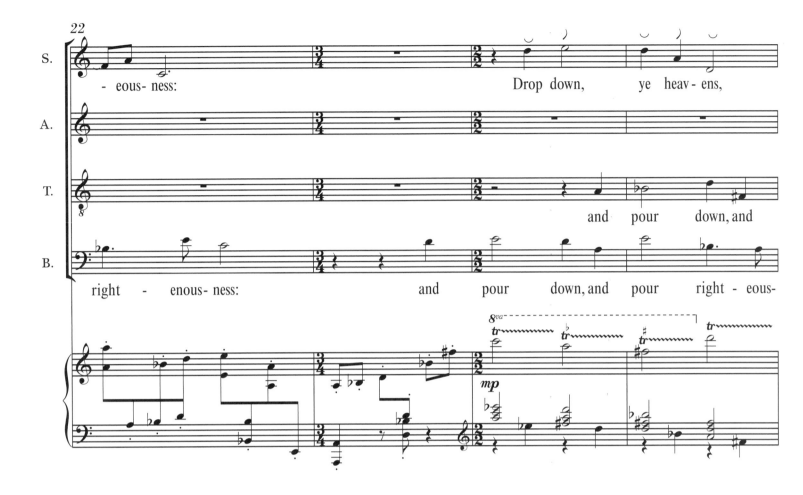

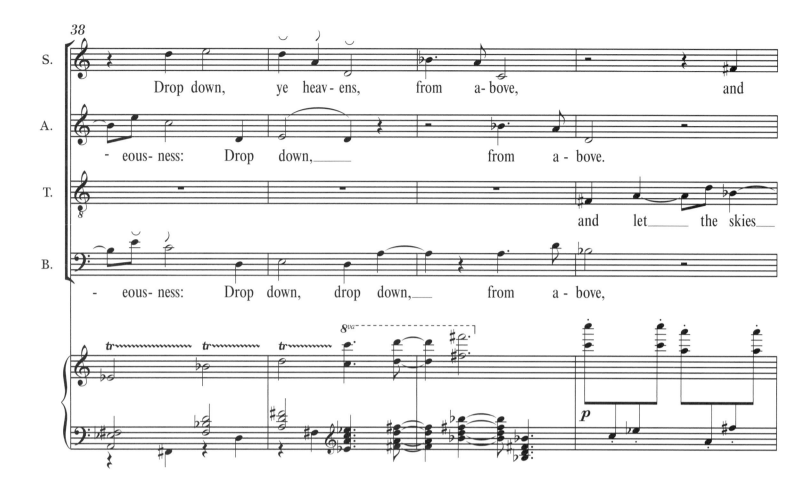

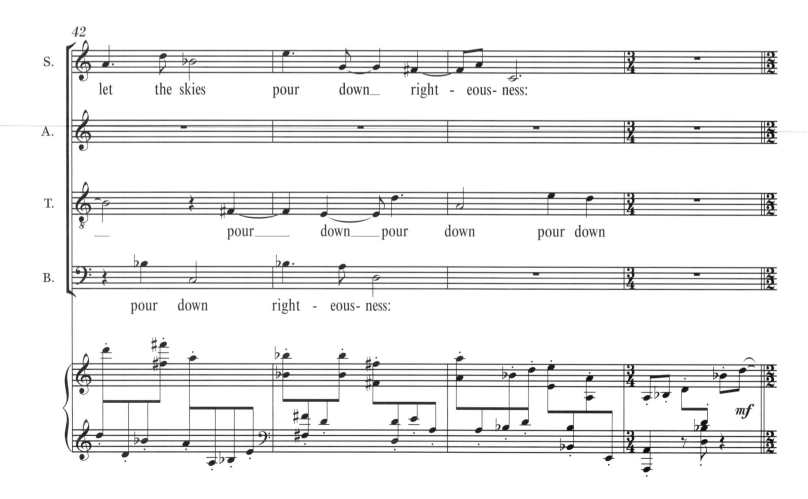

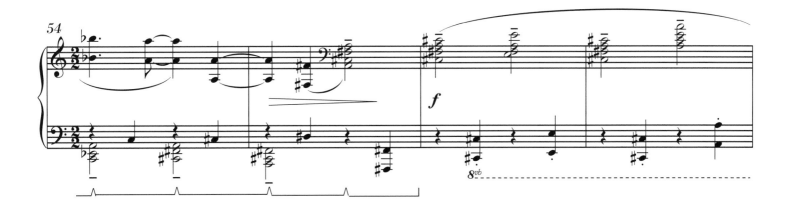

It Is Spring

from The Gospel According
to the Other Mary

Libretto compiled by
PETER SELLARS

Music by
JOHN ADAMS

Piano reduction by
CHITOSE OKASHIRO

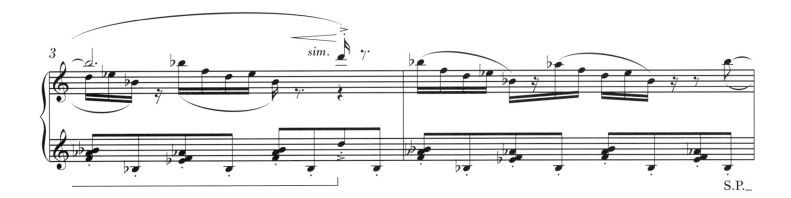

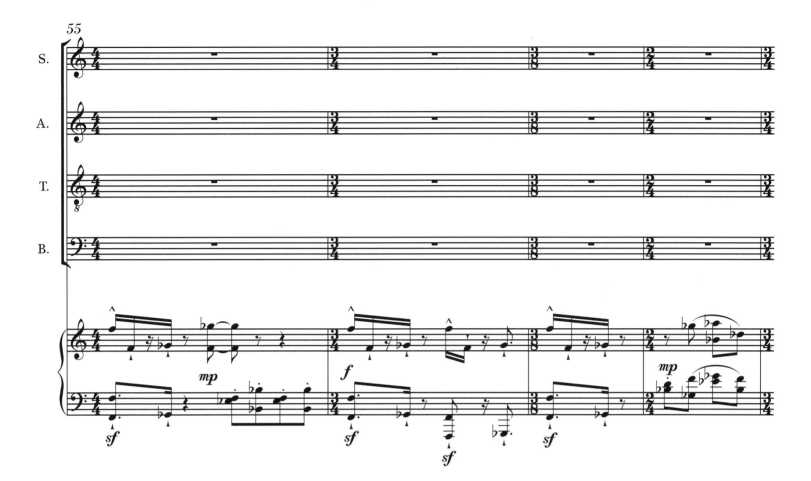

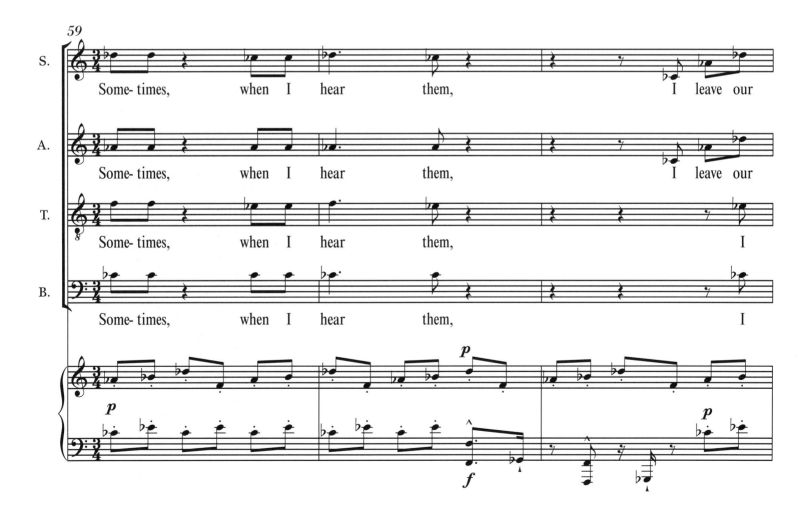

Some- times,   when I hear   them,   I leave our

Some- times,   when I hear   them,   I leave our

Some- times,   when I hear   them,   I

Some- times,   when I hear   them,   I

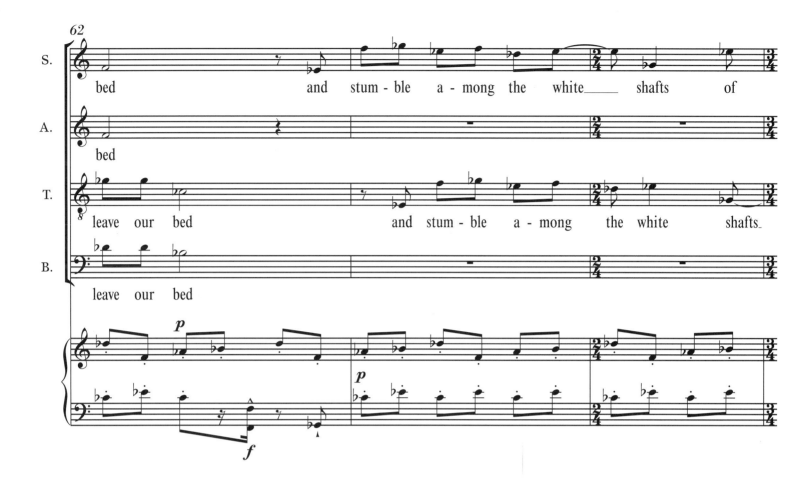

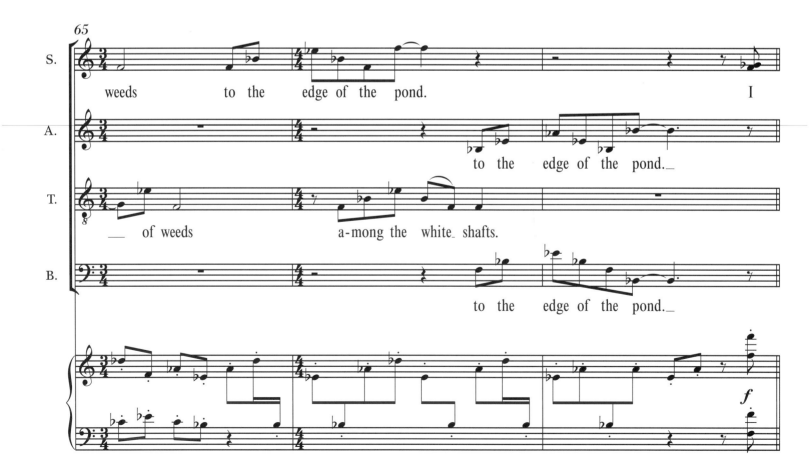

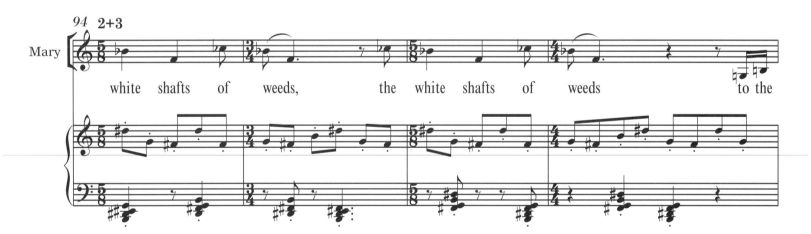

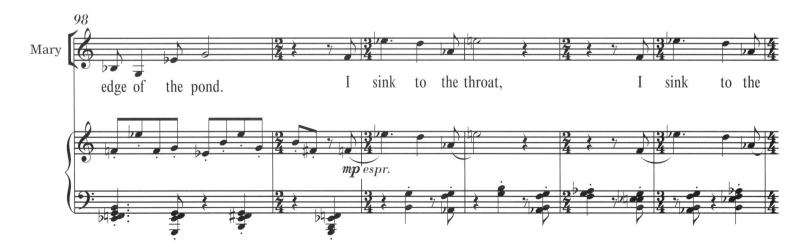

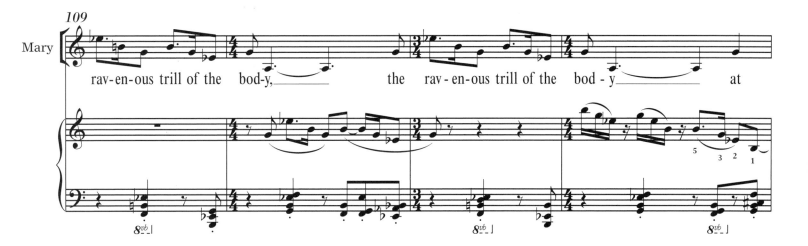

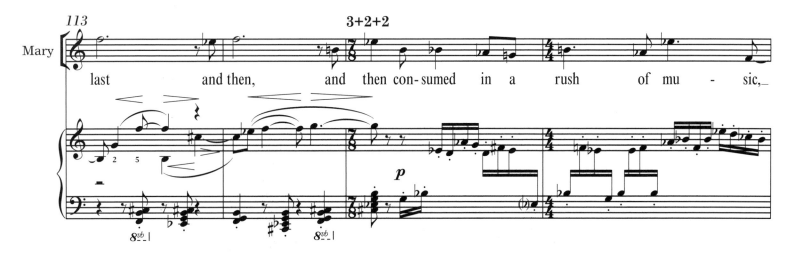

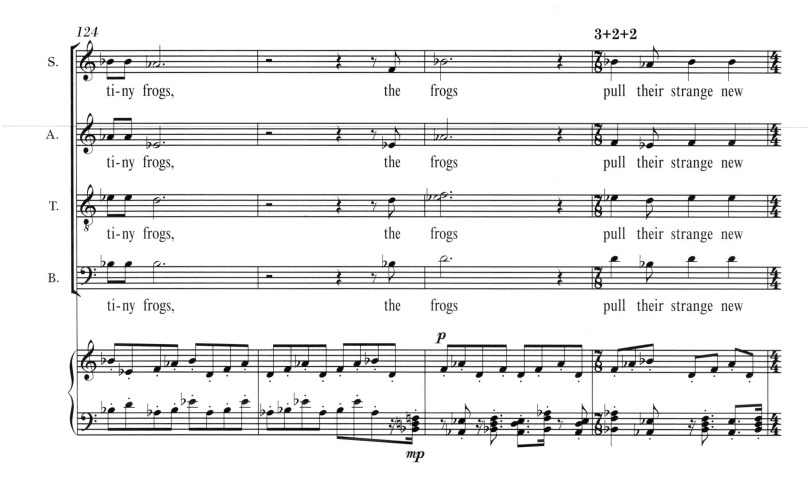

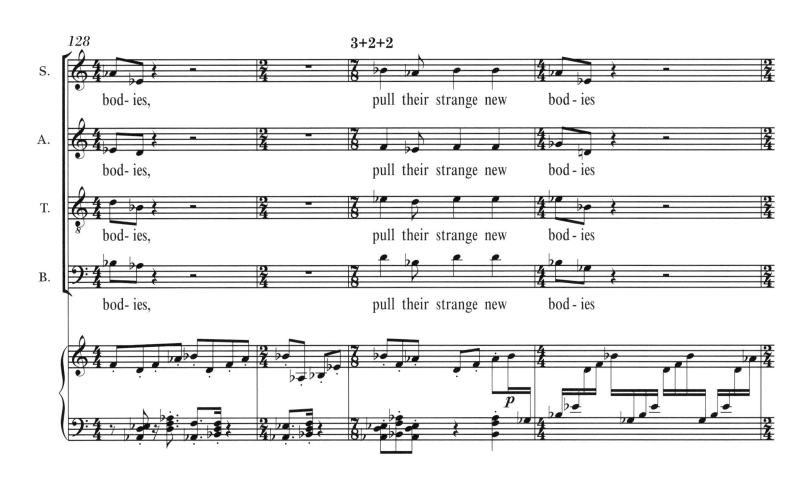

up - ward,   up - ward.

up - ward,   up - ward.

up - ward,   up - ward,

up - ward,   up - ward.

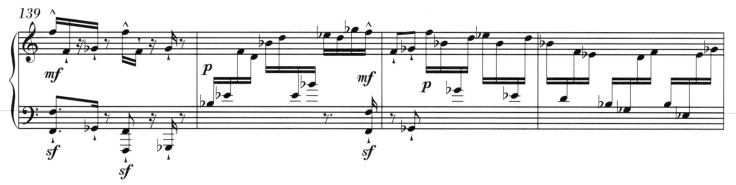

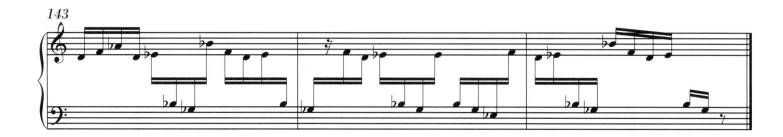